HARD CHOICES

HARD CHOICES

Parenting the Adolescent Child

Eric C. Little, Ph.D., CAADP, ICADC

To order additional copies of this book, contact:
Xlibris Corporation
1-888-795-4274
www.Xlibris.com
Orders@Xlibris.com
49718

CONTENTS

DEDICATION

This book is dedicated to parents everywhere, especially the parents of adolescents. It is my prayer that you will find the encouragement, insight and guidance from these pages that will make your job a little easier, and bring about a closer relationship between you and your teenage son or daughter.

PREFACE

"If you write a book I'll be sure to read it!" These were the words that prompted the writing of this book. They were spoken to me by my youngest daughter's endodontist, after she had undergone a root canal under his skillful hands. Apparently, she had impressed him with her behavior during the visit, being ever so polite and charming. What the good doctor *didn't* see was the emotional roller coaster we rode ever so frequently, the constant struggle to protect her from ungodly influences, and the hard-won battles that had been fought to keep her from going astray.

It was at that point that I decided to accept his challenge of writing a book. It occurred to me that I wasn't the only parent trying to make sense of the adolescent mind. I wasn't the only one who had experienced the kind of love-hate relationship that is so characteristic of parenting during adolescence; and I wasn't the only parent who had experienced calling the police late at night because of a child who hadn't come home, hoping and praying in my heart that she would be found safely.

It is for those of you that have had similar experiences that I write this book. Despite my professional training and experiences, I did not write this book as an "expert." I wrote it, as the apostle John said, as a "companion in tribulation." I wrote it for the purpose of sharing some of the lessons I've learned about this thing called parenting.

A word of thanks is in order to those who helped with this project. I am grateful to Kathy Seifried of the Alabama Department of Mental Health, who gave me the opportunity to share these ideas with others at an ASADS (Alabama School of Alcohol & Drug Studies) Conference. I'd also like to thank my colleague, Dr. Charles Woodley, who took the time to review the clinical aspects of the book and offer helpful suggestions. I must also acknowledge the staff of the Presbyterian Home for Children in Talladega, Alabama. While working with them as a therapist, I witnessed firsthand the extent of their love and devotion to the well-being of the children in their care. Of course, the project would never have materialized without the inspiration of my children, Carol, Erica, Eric II and Jedidah "Rose", who taught me the meaning of parenting, and who enrich my life beyond measure. Finally, I'd like to thank my wife, Rosalind, who provided technical support for the project, and whose love and devotion never cease to amaze me.—Dr. Eric Little

INTRODUCTION

The subject of parenting is a broad one, and there are many aspects of it. This book addresses one aspect of parenting, that of creative discipline. I use the term "creative" because effective parenting requires one to be imaginative and resourceful. It necessitates being able to exercise restraint in the midst of anger and disappointment, and to realize that corporeal punishment is not always the best response to a child's misbehavior. Having said that, I cannot ignore the role that spanking plays in modifying negative behavior. While there are many parents who don't believe in spanking at all, there are times when, in my opinion, spanking can re-direct a child's inappropriate actions, especially if other methods have failed. However, many parents resort to physical discipline because they simply don't know what else to do.

The other thing I should mention in regards to parental discipline is that it should be age appropriate. For instance, spanking may be useful in helping a three year-old understand that it's dangerous to run out into the middle of a busy street, but it is of little benefit to a teenager who is determined to have his way, or who is exhibiting defiant, threatening behavior. This is where the ability to make hard choices comes into play. This book is designed to help parents develop the skills to make those decisions that may in fact be difficult, but necessary.

I have used the phrase *Hard Choices* to describe this approach to parenting the adolescent child. As parents we often find it unpleasant to dispense discipline in any form, and we also find it difficult to make those choices that, in the short run at least, may jeopardize an already strained relationship. Nevertheless, it is the ability to make hard choices that may in fact bring about a more rewarding relationship with our sons and daughters, and in some cases, may even save their lives.

Finally, some words of explanation are in order. In those instances where references to former clients are used, the names are fictitious to ensure confidentiality. In addition, the first chapter contains some information about the neurological changes that contribute to adolescent behavior. My intention was not to inundate the reader with research data, but to share what I think are often overlooked concepts when it comes to adolescent growth and development. Knowledge is power, and knowing what is going on in the mind and body of your teenager is essential to effective parenting.

CHAPTER ONE

The Nature of Adolescence

"I'm straight!" This is the response that I would get from my daughter Erica whenever I asked her how things were going. No, the response had nothing to do with sexual orientation or geometry; it was part of the jargon commonly used in her youth sub-culture. The slang term, as I understood it, meant that things were OK, that her grades were fine, and there were no problems at school. In short, it meant life was good and dad had nothing to worry about. So, when my daughter responded to my query with "I'm straight," it was music to my ears.

But the behavior that is so characteristic of adolescence runs deeper than slang terminology. In fact, recent neurological research supports the idea that it is deeply rooted in the brain. An article published by TIME, focusing on the research of Dr. Jay Giedd, reported that the area of the brain associated with rational thought, planning and organization (the *Prefrontal Cortex*) is the last part of the brain to mature.[1] This may explain why teenagers make impulsive decisions without thinking about consequences. In contrast, research has also discovered that the *Amygdala*, the emotional center of the brain, is more active during adolescence. The Amygdala is also the seat of such emotions as fear and rage. This may explain why teens are often intensely emotional.

Traditional developmental psychology has attributed adolescent behavior to raging hormones. Current research points to a more neurological basis for adolescent behavior. The work of Dr. Jay Giedd and others suggests that the brain goes through a kind of pruning process during adolescence. In other words, the brain produces an excess of brain cells (neurons) and their connections (synapses) prior to puberty. It then begins a pruning process, losing excess neurons and synapses, but strengthening those essential to learning. The implication, Giedd states, is that "If a teen is doing music, sports or academics, those are the connections that will be hard wired. If they're lying on the couch watching MTV or playing video games, those are the cells and connections that are going to survive."[2]

Nevertheless, hormones do play a role in determining what makes adolescents tick. For instance, have you ever been frustrated with trying to get your teen to go to bed at a reasonable hour? Well, the culprit may be the *pineal gland*, which produces the hormone melatonin. Melatonin is a chemical that signals the body to begin shutting down for sleep. In teenagers, it takes longer for melatonin levels to rise. As a result, teens tend to go to bed later and sleep longer than adults. And by the way, alarm clocks don't always provide a viable remedy to this problem! Of course, melatonin is not the only hormone that affects teenage behavior. Other hormones that the pituitary gland releases include the sex hormones testosterone (males) and estrogen (females). Normally, when the level of either hormone in the blood becomes too low, the hypothalamus sends a signal to the pituitary gland to stimulate production of more of that particular hormone. An exception to this rule occurs during puberty, when the sex hormones are released in very large amounts . . . hence the phrase, raging hormones.

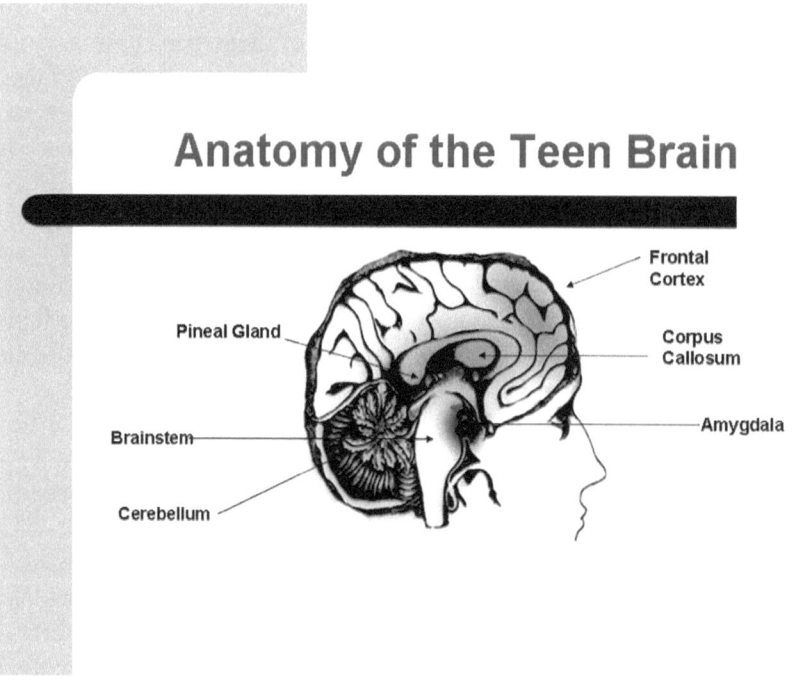

Another important issue that should be included in a discussion of the adolescent brain is that of alcohol and drug abuse. We know that drug abuse is dangerous and costly, both in terms of its damaging impact on the body and the price paid in damaged relationships. Yet, what is often overlooked is the reason *why* so many teenagers get involved with alcohol and drugs in the first place. In addition to the common causal factors such as curiosity, peer pressure, and the desire for acceptance, there are neurological factors as well.

James Bjork of the National Institute on Alcohol Abuse and Alcoholism has been using Functional Magnetic Resonance Imaging (FMRI) to study motivation in adolescents. He suggests that a region of the frontal cortex, called the *nucleus accumbens*, is less active in teenagers than in adults. This region is related to an individual's internal motivation to seek rewards. It appears that the underdevelopment of this region in teens is directly related to their ability (or inability) to delay immediate gratification for long-term rewards. As a result, they are prone to engage in activities that offer high excitement with a low degree of effort, such as experimentation with drugs and alcohol. Once experimentation has begun, the gate is now open for the vicious cycle of addiction to begin; and once addicted, the brain undergoes a kind of transformation. Neurotransmitters, the chemical messengers of the brain, are altered in such a way that one's mood and behavior is affected.

One of the neurotransmitters that play a role in the addictive process is *dopamine.* Addicts become accustomed to high levels of dopamine, which is essential to the regulation of pleasure. Dopamine is manufactured in nerve cells within the ventral tegmental area of the brain and is released in the nucleus accumbens. Under normal circumstances, the dopamine is released via nerve cells in a kind of chain-link fashion to the nucleus accumbens and the frontal cortex. After being released into the synapse (the gap between nerve endings and receiver cells), dopamine binds to the receptors on the next neuron, or nerve cell. The dopamine is either quickly reabsorbed or broken down by the enzyme monoamine oxidase (MAO). Cocaine, for example, blocks the normal absorption of dopamine. As a result, dopamine accumulates in the synapse, where it stimulates the receiver cell. If the cocaine abuser stops taking cocaine, dopamine levels eventually return to normal, but now there are fewer dopamine receptors available to be stimulated. The individual experiences this state as a craving for higher levels of dopamine, leading to a desire for more cocaine.[3]

The longer one is addicted to drugs and/or alcohol, the more harmful the effects on the brain. Many addicts never return to their pre-morbid level of functioning. This helps explain why even some adult addicts behave like adolescents in terms of their impulsivity and poor decision-making.

So what does all this have to do with parenting an adolescent child? First of all, it pays to know what is going on in the mind and body of your teenagers. For sure, we can't stop what's taking place inside them, but we can hold them accountable for their actions and demonstrate patience while the growing pains continue. Secondly, having some knowledge of the psychological and physiological changes that take place during adolescence helps put things in perspective. Let me share with you an example.

When my youngest daughter was in junior high school, I would visit periodically to check on her progress. It was during one of those visits that I noticed a parent in the office who was obviously very frustrated and upset. She had been contacted by the school to bring her son a belt for his pants; and from the looks of things, it was clear to me why he needed one. I then heard her say in a not-so-hushed tone of voice, "This is the *last* time I'm bringing you a belt for your pants!" Evidently, this wasn't the first time her son had gone to school without a belt to hold his pants up. But even if he remembered to wear a belt the next time, there would be something else he'd probably forget to do, like doing his homework before going out to ride his bike with his friends. What this frustrated mom didn't realize was that the part of her son's brain that is responsible for setting priorities and assuming responsibility for certain tasks was not fully developed, and while it made perfect sense to her that he should wear a belt to keep his pants from falling down to his knees, he probably thought he did well enough just to find a pair of pants to put on in the first place.

The above anecdote underscores the importance of exercising patience when parenting adolescent children. The Bible tells us, "He who is slow to wrath has great understanding, but he who is impulsive exalts folly."[4] Just as teenagers must learn how to manage their emotions, so must parents learn the power of restraint. It is much easier to fly off the handle and say things we may later regret, than it is to be patient and gather the facts. And yet, taking the time to gather the facts demonstrates maturity and wisdom that will pay great dividends in your relationship with your teenager. It also provides him or her with a flesh and blood example of what it means to be patient and reasonable when dealing with other people.

Of course, I'm not suggesting that parents do nothing at all when their teens break the rules. Boundaries must be set and teens must be held accountable for their actions; but there comes a time when doing nothing (at least for the moment) is more beneficial. Instead of lashing out verbally or physically in the heat of anger, taking a moment to gather one's thoughts or pray for God's guidance can lead to a more effective course of action. Furthermore, we must realize that there is a thin line between chastisement and abuse. Verbally reprimanding a child for misbehaving is not only appropriate; it is often necessary in order to communicate parental expectations and to discourage negative behavior. However, harsh words that berate and demean may leave emotional scars that last a lifetime. The following poem by Barry Wade, entitled *"Words"* says it best:

Sticks and stones may break my bones, but words can also hurt me.
Stones and sticks break only skin, while words are ghosts that haunt me.
Slant and curved the word-swords fall, to pierce and stick inside me.
Bats and bricks may ache through bones, but words can mortify me.
Pain from words has left its scar on mind and heart and mind that's tender.
Cuts and bruises now have healed; it's words that I remember.

CHAPTER TWO

Pop Culture and Adolescent Behavior

Culture is defined as a group of people who share common values or beliefs; they also share a common language or jargon. Additionally, they experience a collective sense of belonging or loyalty. This definition can be applied not only to races of people but to sub-cultures as well . . . say, adolescents for example.

While it may seem strange to many parents, teenagers today live in a separate sub-culture, complete with their own language (i.e., code words or jargon) and beliefs. Their beliefs encompass things as serious as matters of faith and religion to something seemingly as trivial as their tastes in music. There has always been a kind of cultural divide between parents and their teens, but more recently there appears to be an amoral shift in society's values that is having a profound impact on our children; particularly our teenagers. Dr. Bob Moorehead, former pastor of Seattle's Overlake Christian Church, put it this way:

> *"We spend more, but have less; we buy more, but enjoy less. We have multiplied our possessions, but reduced our values . . . we've added years to life, not life to years. We've been to the moon and back, but have trouble crossing the street to meet a new neighbor. We conquered outer space, but not inner space. We've done larger things, but not better things. We've cleaned up the air, but polluted the soul . . . conquered the atom, but not our prejudices. These are days of quick trips, disposable diapers, throwaway morality and one night stands."*

Most of us over 40 can remember a time when the family unit was the building block of society. That is, most of the moral values we learned as children were taught at home. These values of right and wrong were reinforced at school, church, and in our communities, and helped shape our worldview as adults. The problem we now face in America is that other societal influences have a tremendous impact on the attitudes and behaviors of our teens, while the influences of home appear to be waning. Indeed, there are thousands of teenagers who have no stable home life; and many lose themselves to the influences of drugs, crime, prostitution and gang-related activity. The family unit, once viewed as the centerpiece of society, is under great pressure to survive. This drift in societal values has had a residual effect on the attitudes and behaviors of many teenagers, and has placed an enormous strain on family life.

The diagram below illustrates how the family unit should be the centerpiece of society. The white circle surrounding the family unit represents the major social institutions that influence the behavior of children within the family unit (e.g., educational, religious, and political institutions). Parental values and beliefs also have a tremendous impact on the values and beliefs of their children. These values are internalized over time, and when the children become adults, they incorporate those values into their everyday lives. They are then in a position to influence others in the wider society, hopefully for the better.

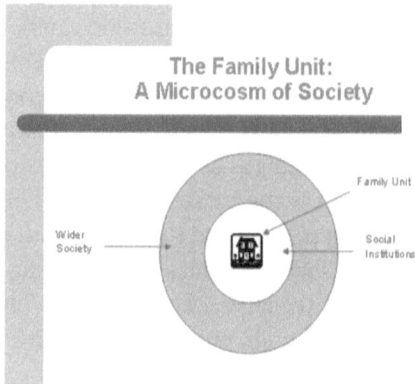

The shift we are seeing is that the wider society appears to exert *more* influence on the family unit (teens in particular) through mediums such as TV and radio, and commercial marketing schemes directed at young minds. The results are sometimes alarming. Teenagers and pre-teens alike are becoming more and more materialistic, while values such as empathy, self-sacrifice, and compassion for the less fortunate are disappearing. Researcher Sharon Beder explains it this way: "In their early teens, children are forming their own identities and they are highly vulnerable to pressure to conform to group standards and mores. Advertising manipulates them through their insecurities, seeking to define normality for them, and undermining fundamental human values. Advertisements actively encourage them to seek happiness and esteem through consumption."[5]

The waning influence of traditional values among teens was made painfully clear to me during a presentation I gave several years ago at a large high school in Alabama.

I had planned to talk about the psychological and health-related benefits of sexual abstinence until marriage, and began the discussion by asking, "How many of you would like to get married someday?" Fewer than twenty percent of the group assembled that day raised their hands, most of which were teenage girls. Out of concern as well as curiosity, I queried the group to find out why the idea of marriage was not appealing to them. Their answers were honest and compelling. One fifteen year-old spoke of the violence inflicted upon her mother during an abusive relationship that eventually ended in divorce. Others came from broken homes were there was little, if any, male presence, and marriage was never an expectation.

I realized then and there that marriage was not something that many teens looked forward to.

The concept of marriage is further dissipated by sit-coms and TV shows that imply that it's OK for couples to live together without the commitment of marriage. In fact, many TV shows seem to infer that cohabitation and the accompanying sexual relations between partners in such a relationship is the norm rather than the exception, and that there need be no spiritual or legal ties. It seems that marriage as a viable social institution is fast becoming a relic of the past; but not without consequences.

A study done by the National Marriage Project at Rutgers University concluded that couples that live together without the ceremony of marriage have an increased risk of breaking up afterward. In addition, the absence of the marital bond makes it easier for couples to call it quits, since there are no spiritual or legal considerations. As Katie Roiphe puts it, "You don't have the idea of the future stretching out ahead of you . . . you don't have the romantic momentum of marriage. In a way you have the worst of both worlds; routine without stability, lack of freedom without commitment." [6] I am not suggesting that marriage is a panacea, nor am I suggesting that men or women in an abusive marital relationship should remain in that relationship at any cost. However, I do believe that the shift away from marriage contributes to the instability of the family unit and may have far-reaching effects on generations unborn.

The Influence of Pop Music and the Entertainment Industry

There is another, perhaps more subtle influence upon teens, and that is the influence of popular music. I use the phrase "subtle influence" because oftentimes parents are unaware of the kinds of music their teens listen to. The influence is also subtle in that the lyrics of many popular songs (including rap, hip hop, rock, etc) encourage sexual promiscuity, vengeful violence, and defiance of adult authority. Many music videos are little more than pornographic exhibitions that glamorize a life of pleasure seeking, partying, and materialism. Of course, there are many artists who write songs and produce music videos with positive messages. They are not the focus of my concern.

As parents, it is very easy to turn a deaf ear to the music our children listen to, and pass it off as just a "phase" they're going through. It may indeed be a phase, but we are responsible, in large part, for how they mature and the values they adopt during the stage of adolescence. Misty Bernall, the mother of Cassie Bernall (one of the students killed during the Columbine Massacre), provides a poignant illustration of the need for parents to be aware of the music their teens listen to. In her book, *She Said Yes,* Mrs. Bernall recounts a chilling episode in Cassie's life prior to the transformation that gave her the courage to die a martyr's death. She describes it this way:

> "I don't know exactly when it was, but at some point we began examining some of Cassie's music and realized that it wasn't just entertainment. Despite the innocuous covers, the lyrics themselves carried an unmistakable message." She goes on to quote lyrics from a Marilyn Manson song, which was one of Cassie's favorites at the time. The song was also a favorite of Harris and Klebold, the two students who went on a murderous rampage that fateful day at Columbine High: "*I bash myself to sleep . . . what you sow I will reap. I scar myself you will see; I wish I wasn't me. I throw a little fit . . . I slit my teenage wrist. But your selective judgments and good-guy badges don't mean a f—to me . . . get your gun, get your gun.*"[7]

I'll discuss Cassie's spiritual journey in more detail in a later chapter, but what is interesting about this time in Cassie's life is that she had begun to self-mutilate. It was also a time of intense conflict with her parents. In fact, it was the discovery of notes written to Cassie by a teenage friend (suggesting that they kill her parents) that prompted the Bernalls' closer examination of their daughter's taste in music. And while I concede that music alone does not create a murderer, I do believe that it can exert negative influences that impact teenage behavior. Consider the lyrics to Eminem's "My Name Is":

> "*Hi kids! Do you like violence? Wanna see me stick nine inch nails through one of my eyelids? Wanna copy me and do exactly like I did? Try acid and get f—ed up worse than my life is? Well since age twelve, I've felt like I'm someone else, cause I hung my original self from the top bunk with a belt . . . I smoke a fat pound of grass and fall on my ass, faster than a fat b—who sat down too fast.*"

Or consider the lyrics of "Juicy J" and Three Six Mafia: "*I gotta 357 brand new—shootin' holes through. Let's get da dope and drop it off and count them G's and smoke some cheese . . . it pays to break the law.*" Other titles on Three 6 Mafia's album, *Hypnotize Camp Posse* includes songs such as "Don't Make Me Kill" and

"D—k Sucking Ho's." These are just a sample of the rap group's genre. I will not take the space here to provide the lyrics to these songs, but I'm sure you get the picture. Amazingly, in March 2006 the group won an Academy Award for the song: "It's Hard Out Here for a Pimp."

Harmless? Some people may think so, including your average teenager. However, the references to violence, promiscuity and drug abuse in songs such as the ones I described are clear. Even if one argues that lyrics such as these do not incite violence and drug abuse, it is apparent that the shock value inherent in these songs has a way of numbing the minds of young people in a way that makes such behavior perversely acceptable. And it's not just the music industry. Video gaming is big business in America, and many teens spend countless hours playing video games on their X-Boxes. Yet, it doesn't seem to matter that the recurrent theme in games such as Doom II and Grand Theft Auto is violence, lawlessness and revenge. Bob Larson put it best when he wrote, "Children are accustomed to seeing heads severed by sabers, bullets tearing through flesh in slow motion, and blood spurting from disassembled appendages. The message is easy to understand: killing is glorious."[8]

That message is underscored by the number of lawsuits that have recently been filed against the makers of games like Grand Theft Auto. One such lawsuit involved 18 year-old Devin Moore, who gunned down two police officers and a radio dispatcher in the small town of Fayette, Alabama. According to news reports, Moore was arrested in 2003 for stealing a car. Once inside the police station, he "snapped" and grabbed the booking officer's gun and shot him twice. He then turned and shot another officer three times, and on the way out, shot the dispatcher five times. After his capture, Moore reportedly told police, "Life is like a video game; everybody's got to die sometime." It was later revealed that Moore had purchased Grand Theft Auto as a minor and had literally spent hundreds of hours playing the game prior to his crime spree.

The evidence connecting pop music and entertainment to teenage behavior is more than anecdotal or subjective. In one PRIDE survey, 2% of 4th graders reported carrying a gun to school, 4% reported carrying a knife. A full 32% reported having been assaulted while at school. By the time students reached the 12th grade, one out of four reported monthly illicit drug use.[9] The national scope of the impact of entertainment media on children was highlighted at a recent Subcommittee Hearing on Telecommunications in Washington D.C. It was there that the chairman of communications for the American Academy of Pediatrics, Dr. Donald Shifrin stated, "Music videos, movies, video games and television has displaced parents as the primary influence in their [children's] lives." He went on to point out that "one-third of children younger than six years old have a television set in their bedroom." The impact of popular music and other forms of entertainment media on our youth can hardly be ignored.

CHAPTER THREE

Remember the Difference

I first heard this phrase when listening to Milton Creagh, a well-known youth speaker. His point was succinct but one that is often overlooked by parents today; that there *is* a difference between parents and their children, between adults and teenagers. The difference is not only chronological in terms of age, but is also physiological and psychological. This difference is reflected in the laws that govern the social, legal and educational rights of children.

Even if your teenager doesn't think so, there is a reason that children under a certain age cannot work full-time, vote, drive or engage in other adult activities. There is a reason that children are legally expected to attend school until a certain age; it gives them the opportunity to learn crucial life skills, to understand the meaning of commitment, and to prepare themselves socially, educationally and financially for their future. No matter how much teenagers *feel* like they are an adult, or *believe* that they deserve adult privileges, the fact of the matter is that they lack the life experiences necessary for successful living.

They also lack the financial stability to live a quality life; and unless they prepare themselves academically, they will often have to rely on menial jobs to sustain themselves. That is why the role of parents and responsible adults is so important; we can provide the guidance necessary to help the young people in our lives mature and become successful adults; provided they are willing to listen and take heed to wise counsel. When they are not willing to listen to sound advice, or choose paths that lead to destruction, it becomes obvious that there is a difference between adults and children; for it is then that their choices often require adult intervention to steer them back on track, sometimes to prevent even more negative consequences. It is at that time that hard choices must be made.

For instance, if a parent knows that his teenage son is using illicit drugs, he should not feel obligated to give him money just because he asks for it. If a teenage daughter is doing poorly in school when she has the potential to do better, her parents should not continue to give her the freedom to hang out with her friends or drive the car. Of course, once you put your foot down and say "no" there will be plenty of huffing and puffing. But remember God holds you, the parent, responsible for shaping, guiding and molding that teenager of yours into a mature adult. You are probably familiar with the proverb, "Train up a child in the way he should go, and when he is old he will not depart from it."[10] God did not promise it would be easy. Stand your ground and be willing to make hard choices.

I made reference earlier to the importance of school attendance. While it is not the primary goal of educational institutions to teach morality, schools nonetheless provide a kind of testing ground for spiritual and moral convictions. Peer pressure is real, and many adolescents, particularly in the middle and high school years, feel the pressure (openly or subtly) to conform. This is why it is important for children to develop a moral compass early in life; to be able to distinguish between right and wrong. It is very common among teens to do something simply because someone else is doing it, or to want something because someone else has it. And much of the doing and wanting is the result of a need to belong, to fit in, or to feel accepted.

At some point, teens must realize that they do not have to be defined by material possessions, fashion images, or foolish expectations of bravado; they can be satisfied with the knowledge that they are loved and valued by others, and that their uniqueness is their strength. Again, this is a lesson that adults can impart to the teenagers in their lives. As adults, we often become exasperated with this adolescent obsession with peer conformity. I admit, it is difficult to distance ourselves totally from the fashion industry, music industry and other teen-targeted industries. Our children need clothes and shoes to wear, music or other forms of entertainment to occupy their time, and food to eat. But I think the saving grace is in reaching some kind of balance; providing for their needs while at the same time teaching them the importance of restraint and individuality. They must learn that they cannot have everything they want when they want it. Even if parents can afford to give their children everything they want, they send the wrong message when they give in to every adolescent whim. Materialistic over-indulgence leads to the development of a selfish, demanding personality that people love to hate.

The Friendship Factor

Somewhere along the way, we were given the notion that we should strive to be friends to our children. Now, I'm not saying that this is a totally bad idea, but friendship and parenting are not necessarily one and the same. I can befriend someone without the responsibilities that come with being a parent. I can be your friend without feeding you, clothing you, taking you to the doctor when you're sick, or teaching you the difference between right and wrong. Yes, any one of those things may become necessary during the course of a friendship, but they are not expected, nor are they really required. But they *are* expected of a parent, and they are required if we intend to be the best parents we can be.

This can be a hard choice for some parents. For some reason, there are those parents who are afraid to administer discipline when it's desperately needed. They are afraid to set boundaries and limits even when it's clear that the child's behavior is detrimental to his own well being. Perhaps one of the reasons is because they (the parents) were abused and mistreated as children, so they grow up determined to treat their children differently. This is understandable, but some parents take this idea to the extreme and administer hardly any discipline at all. Others fear that their children will reject them, or that they will somehow lose the affection of their children if they discipline them. To the contrary, children come to appreciate loving discipline, because it says "I care about you."

Take Dennis, for example. At age six he was in residential care because of parental neglect. At an interview he confided, "They let me do whatever I want." And yet, he favored residential care over living with his parents because he had come to appreciate daily structure and loving discipline. Unlike the chaos of his home environment, there were rules to follow and boundaries to respect. Responsibility was taught by giving him chores appropriate for his age. Even at age six, he could recognize that the structure of residential care was better than living in a home where there was freedom without responsibility.

But does this work for teenagers? The answer is *yes*. Sandra, a sixteen year-old who also lived in residential care is another example. I had the privilege of working with Sandra for about three months before she was placed with a relative. I'll never forget what she said to me during our last session together: *"When I first came here I thought I was tough . . . thought I knew it all. But since I've been here I've learned what it means to be loved . . . to be cared for. I truly believe God allowed me to go through this experience."*

Like most teens, Sandra thought she was invincible. She had already experienced what most parents fear. She was sexually active and had experimented with drugs and alcohol. When we first met, she announced that she was an atheist and had no use for God. However, she was also filled with anxiety and expressed a deep-seated fear of death and dying. Before she left residential care she had acquired a vibrant faith, and death no longer frightened her. Her transformation was due in large part to the unconditional love she received and to an environment where there were boundaries as well as consequences for negative behavior. In short, she came to realize that there was a difference between adults and children.

For sure, teens are caught up in a kind of emotional purgatory. They want to experience the adult world, and in many aspects they are physically capable of doing so. However, most lack the emotional maturity to see the long-range consequences of their behavior. Take for instance the girl who agrees to have sex with her boyfriend and unexpectedly becomes pregnant. Add to this scenario that she is in the 11th or 12th grade when this happens and eventually drops out of school to take care of the baby. Because of her family's limited income, she is now forced to work to help provide for herself and her child. Even though she wants to finish her high school education, she is shackled by responsibility and never seems to get around to it. Ten years later, unless she has determined to improve her circumstances, she will still be working for minimum wage and struggling to make ends meet. This scenario is all too common among teens. As parents and helping professionals, we must help our young women (and men) understand that there is a difference between adolescence and adulthood. Using the example above, it makes a huge difference in a woman's life to have a child *after* she's finished high school or college. Every rung climbed on the educational ladder also increases one's economic opportunities, which in turn make it easier to provide for a child's material needs.

While we are on the subject of teen sexuality, I personally believe that teens should wait until they're married to have sex, or at least until they establish a monogamous (having only one partner) relationship. Abstinence not only carries spiritual and emotional benefits, it also reduces the likelihood of sexually transmitted diseases; including HIV. However, I realize that we live in a world where more and more adolescents are becoming sexually active (at younger ages), and to avoid discussions about birth control or responsible sexual activity is to place them at risk. Parents should not be afraid to talk honestly with their teens about sex, and to make them aware that they can choose to abstain from sexual activity until they develop a stable relationship with someone of the opposite sex, as in marriage. Even if they are already sexually active, there is something called *secondary virginity*. Once they understand the emotional and health risks that go along with sexual activity, they can choose to remain abstinent until a monogamous relationship can be established.

Chapter Four

The Art of Making Hard Choices

I refer to the making of hard choices as an "art," because the act of making sound parental decisions requires a certain amount of skill, as well as a healthy dose of faith. Indeed, many of the choices we make concerning our teens are made by faith. That is, we are not really sure if the decisions we make at any given time will turn out the way we hope. Given the options before us and the certainty that things will get worse if we *don't* act, we are prompted as parents to take leaps of faith without the benefit of hindsight. We trust in the promise of Romans 8:28: *"And we know all things work together for good to those who love God; to those who are called according to His purpose."*

Nevertheless, our skills as parents are honed as we continue to balance the act of unconditional love and creative discipline. One of the principles that helped me in the rearing of my own children was discovered years ago while reading Jay Adams' book, *Competent to Counsel.* It was here that I came across the principle that Adams described as "yanking and oozing."

In the context of counseling, the term "yanking" refers to instances when the clinician may have to confront the client with his or her own self-defeating attitudes and behaviors, which have contributed to the client's personal problems. The counselor respectfully but firmly breaks down the wall of denial behind which the client has been hiding, thus "yanking" the client into the reality of the need for change. On the other hand, there are times when such a confrontational approach would do more harm than good. For some clients, a more subtle approach is necessary. Instead of "yanking," the client is gradually brought into the realization that change is needed, and the clinician guides the client through the process of making those needed changes. Adams describes this process as "oozing."

So it is with our children. For the "strong-willed" child, a direct, confrontational approach may be needed. Unfortunately, many parents are afraid to confront. Even in counseling circles, the term *confrontation* has become a dirty word. But this is unfortunate, because in refusing to confront, we communicate that we are afraid, or that we just don't care. Some have referred to this act of confrontation as "tough love." Whatever you call it, it is a necessary part of parenting the adolescent child; especially the child who is strong-willed, defiant or critical of parental authority.

I remember when my son was about sixteen; he had obtained his driver's license and was allowed to drive one of our vehicles. Unknown to me (until I happened to find a traffic ticket lying around), he had been ticketed for speeding and other moving violations, and had accumulated a substantial number of fines. When I confronted him with this, he chose to shift the blame to *me* by implying that I cared more about the fines than for him, which was not the real issue. The issue at hand was his disregard for law and order, and his lack of honesty in telling us about the violations. He became furious when I told him to hand over the keys, and he then announced that he was leaving home. Despite the fear and uncertainty that swelled within me, I didn't stop him from leaving. He left home the same day.

What followed were several months of sitting on pins and needles. Occasionally he would call to speak with his mother, but he avoided talking to me. He wouldn't tell us where he was, so I filed a missing person's report with the police. I'll never forget the day I took my son's photo to the police precinct and the ache I felt in my heart as I admitted that my son was somewhere roaming the streets, refusing to come home. Not knowing what else to do, and fearing for his safety and well-being, I turned him over to God in prayer . . . then one day the phone rang. My wife answered; I could tell it was my son on the other end. They conversed for a short time and I heard her say to him, "You need to talk to your dad." She handed over the phone and, although I don't recall the entire conversation, I remember the following exchange:

> *"Dad, how did it come to this?"*
> "It was the choices you made, son."
> *"What am I to do?"*
> "You can come back home."

We talked some more, but the end result of our conversation was that my son returned home, completed his high school education and later, to my surprise, answered the call to Christian Ministry. He is now married to a lovely young woman and proudly serving his country in the United States Army. There is much more I could add to this story, but suffice it to say that, had I not been willing to confront, the story may not have had a happy ending. Now, I'm not suggesting that every parent make the choice that I made in that particular situation, but given the alternatives, I felt I needed to stand my ground. I am grateful that God allowed the situation to work together for our good.

CHAPTER FIVE

Effective Parenting Tips

There are many books and periodicals that provide parenting tips. However, the concepts that I present here are geared toward helping parents deal with adolescence; that "rough and tumble" phase of child growth and development that leaves parents searching for concrete ways to help them cope with teenage behavior. While you may not need to utilize all of these, feel free to use any that you feel appropriate given the situation at hand. Keep in mind that some of these tips may involve doing things that you've never tried before; you may in fact be stepping outside your comfort zone. Remember, however, that if what you've tried before hasn't worked, you've got nothing to lose; it's all about making hard choices.

- *Don't castrastrophize.* Parenting is difficult enough without turning small anthills into giant mounds. I have known cases where parents go ballistic when a child brings home a "C" on a report card. While we all want our children to succeed, it is counter-productive to over-exaggerate a situation that may not be as bad as it seems.

- *Communicate openly & frequently.* I advocate something called "The Open Door Approach." That is, create an atmosphere in which your teenager feels comfortable coming to you to talk about things . . . anything! In the fit of anger or frustration, a child may retreat to his or her room and bawl. If the parent is unaware of the cause of the teen's frustration, the temptation is to find out what's going on right then and there, even though your child may not be ready or willing to talk about it. The hard thing to do is back off, express concern, and "leave the door open" for your teen to talk about it later; even if you're the one to initiate the conversation.

- *Ask open-ended questions.* Another key ingredient of open communication is initiating dialogue. Questions like, "How was your day?" generally evoke a response such as "OK" or "Fine." Instead, ask questions like, "Did anything interesting happen to you at school today?" Or "How are things going between you and . . . ?" The theme may vary, but the idea is to generate meaningful conversation that requires more than a "yes or no" answer.

- **Control your fears.** Every parent gets nervous when curfew hits and your teens are not home. Resist the urge to pick up the phone and nag. Instead, give them a few minutes to prove themselves. There are times when things happen beyond their control. For example, they may be riding with a friend who makes an unexpected stop, or despite their good intentions, they may lose track of time. Tell your teens to call you if they see where they're going to be late getting home. If you begin to see a pattern of disregard for curfew, address the issue, and don't be afraid to let limits or say "no" if needed. The point here is to not allow your fears and anxieties to get the best of you. Most of our worst fears never materialize anyway.

- **Inspect and expect.** Take time to periodically look in your teenager's room to catch a glimpse of what he or she is about. Look at the walls to see what pop star is admired; pay attention to the music that is played. Don't be afraid to share your values; teenagers are still developing values of their own, and it's important for them to know what you think. I'm not suggesting that parents routinely invade their teen's privacy, but it's neither wise nor helpful to you as a parent to be unaware of what's going on under your own roof. Internet technology has both the capacity for good and evil, and many teenage girls have been lured away by predators on the Internet. If your teen spends an inordinate amount of time on the Internet, periodically browse the search engines to see what they're interested in. You may be surprised at what you find.

At the same time, set expectations for your adolescent son or daughter. Let them know that you have faith in them, and that you do not expect them to betray your trust. If they lie to you or in some other way prove themselves untrustworthy, let them know how you feel, and be prepared to set consequences in motion. It is the nature of adolescence to "push the envelope," but if teens have a clear understanding of what is expected of them, accepting the consequences of negative behavior becomes easier, and in turn makes life easier for you, the parent.

- **Say "yes" more often.** Oftentimes parents say "no" because they can. Sometimes our irrational fears dictate our response, and at other times it's simply *easier* to refuse a teenager's request, especially when answering "yes" creates an inconvenience for us. However, arbitrary refusal of a teen's request may lead to hidden resentment, which can ultimately lead to defiant behavior. It may also cause the teenager to find ways to get out of the house *without* your permission, which can have implications for the child's safety. There is wisdom in the Apostle Paul's admonition to fathers, which is applicable to parents in general: *"And now a word to you fathers. Don't make your children angry by the way you treat them. Rather, bring them up with the discipline and instruction approved by the Lord."*[11]

- *Take advantage of opportunities to build character.* As adults we sometimes forget that we were children once, and that someone took the time to teach us important lessons of life. Even when it comes to completing household chores, we are often tempted to criticize our children when they don't meet our expectations. But sometimes we fail to realize how hard children try to please their parents. If they fail to meet our standards, it may not be the result of indifference or an unwillingness to comply. It may be that they simply don't possess the experience to do the job as well as we'd like. In some instances, their brains interpret instructions differently than ours; so the three-step instructions we thought were simple don't always come across that way to adolescents. So if your teen doesn't mow the lawn perfectly the first time, don't sweat it, he may get better with practice! Remember, it's not about getting the job done, it's about building character.

- *Don't go it alone.* Parenting is difficult enough without trying to be a superhero. Don't be afraid to share your parenting experiences with other parents you trust. If the relationship between you and your teenager is especially strained, or if there are safety concerns, don't be ashamed to seek professional help. All too often, families suffer because parents want to maintain the image of a "perfect" family in the community. Or, they are fearful of the stigma associated with seeking the help of a mental health professional. The truth is, we are all human, and no amount of money, education or social status exempts us from life's problems; especially when it comes to this thing called parenting.

- *Utilize peer influence.* Believe it or not, parents are not the only ones that exert influence on teenage behavior. In fact, there are other significant persons in your child's life that may have even more influence on your child. That person could be a friend or relative whom the child respects or admire. The important thing to remember is that it doesn't matter who exerts a positive influence on your teen, just be willing to use that influence to your advantage.

I remember when my youngest daughter and I were going through a rather difficult period in our relationship. It seemed that no matter what I did or said, nothing seemed to work to curtail her self-destructive behavior. Well, one day several of her closest friends came over to visit, and I shared my concerns with them, partly out of exasperation, and partly because I knew they cared for her; and that if they knew the whole story they would hold her accountable for her actions. Fortunately, these were friends whose parents I knew, who had been instilled with a sense of right and wrong. They confronted her about her behavior, and before long, I had my daughter back.

- *Listen with your heart.* Years ago, John Drakeford wrote a book entitled, *The Awesome Power of the Listening Heart.* In the book, he discusses the impact that good listening can have on relationships. He also laments the fact that too few people understand that listening involves more than just *hearing* what another person is saying; it also involves reading "between the lines" to uncover subtle, yet important messages. So it is with our children. All too often, parents and adults fail to listen closely to youthful concerns. What may seem insignificant to an adult can be extremely important to an adolescent. As a result, the concerns and emotional needs of children are often brushed aside with a quick remark or an empty promise that leaves the child feeling frustrated and misunderstood.

- *Be generous with praise.* Complimenting a child for a job well done may seem like an obvious thing to do, but the reality is that many parents fail to do it often enough. It seems that scolding, criticizing and reprimanding are "normal" responses to a child's misbehavior or failed attempt to complete certain tasks. It takes more effort, however, to find something praiseworthy. The impact of a positive comment or word of encouragement goes much farther than any criticism. It helps build self-esteem, and makes children more eager to do those things that will earn them praise from caring adults.

- *Know who your teen hangs out with.* I admit it's hard to keep up with a teenager's friends, especially when the entire family is "on the go." In addition, some parents may feel as if they're intruding into their children's lives by asking them about every friend or acquaintance that comes around. Nevertheless, it is very important to know who your child's friends are. Not only is it important to know their names, but you should also make it a point to know where they live and obtain phone numbers as well. Getting to know some of the parents of the teens your children hang out with is also very helpful. Unfortunately, we live in an age in which internet predators and child molesters are prevalent in society, and in the event your child should run away or become missing, having this information may be the key to finding them.

- **Be flexible with rules.** Adolescents encounter rules from a variety of sources, but most of them are generated at home or at school. Teenagers need structure and guidance; however, in many instances, enforcement of rules becomes an end in itself. This is especially true in organizations and institutions that serve the adolescent population. Parents and adults in authority should understand that compliance with rules should not supersede development of character, and that the element of compassion should be included when it comes to adherence to organizational or parental rules.

- **Don't give up.** This may seem redundant, since most of us would never give up on our children, no matter how difficult things get. However, there are those parents who have struggled so long and so hard, that they literally get to a point where they don't have the emotional resources to go any further. Their apparent lack of concern is not due to apathy but rather exhaustion. They have cried, counseled, argued, disciplined and gone to great lengths to save their teenage son or daughter; only to endure one heartbreak too many, or to watch their teen become entangled in the criminal justice system. Even so, I encourage parents to take heart, for you never know what life experience will bring your child to the realization that he has pushed the envelope too far; and like the prodigal son, will ask for forgiveness and reconciliation.

- **Don't underestimate the power of prayer.** In the realm of human relationships, there is only so much we can do. Attempts to force change upon people often end in disaster, with relationships becoming even more strained and distant. This is where prayer comes in. God can "turn the hearts of parents to their children, and the hearts of children to their parents" (Malachi 4:5b). Nevertheless, it is hard for some people to resort to prayer because they are "fixers." That is, they feel that they have to *do something* to remedy the situation. It's difficult for them to realize that there are some situations that defy human efforts and require divine intervention. Of course, you do what you can to keep your child from destroying his life, even if it means legal intervention. But the legal system is not perfect; neither does it provide perfect answers to complex situations. Prayer can be the key to unlock the doors of restoration and deliverance.

CHAPTER SIX

The Emotional Roller Coaster

I don't like roller-coasters. I know they're a lot of fun for people who like thrills and screams, but I tend to avoid them now that I'm older. Perhaps I lost my enthusiasm the last time I rode one at Six Flags in Atlanta; the time when a really nice wristwatch went flying off my wrist into the wild blue yonder. I've never been back on one since.

Parenting teens is a lot like riding a roller coaster; the emotional ups and downs, the times of extreme excitement and utter disappointment. Unlike the ones at amusement parks however, for parents of adolescents, riding this emotional roller coaster is not an option. It is a part of living with and being involved in the life of a teenager. What's more, even the teens that make up the ride are often frustrated by their emotional highs and lows. They know their bodies and minds are undergoing changes, but they sometimes feel helpless in terms of what to do to make the transition easier.

When my youngest daughter became upset and tearful over the fact that her older siblings were experiencing the freedom that comes with driving, working (i.e., having your own money), and going places with their friends, I reminded her that with freedom comes responsibility. I also reminded her that, because of her age, there were several years of frustration still to come, and that she might as well get used to the fact that she would not be able to do everything she wanted to do or have everything she wanted. Fortunately, she internalized that message. And even though she was still on the roller coaster, her attitude was different. She took her disappointments in stride, and seemed to be no worse for the wear.

As I mentioned earlier, I think the mistake some parents make is that they try to give their children *everything*. For sure, all good parents want to provide for their children and give them the best that life affords. We must remember, however, that too much too soon can spoil a child. We have heard the old adage, "Spare the rod; spoil the child." Well, today it is not the sparing of the rod (withholding corporeal punishment) that spoils many children; it is the refusal to withhold materialistic gifts. We live in a society in which some parents measure their self-esteem by the price of the shoes on their child's feet. In an effort to keep up with the latest fad, they have created materialistic young people who expect to get (and often do) everything they want.

For many of you reading this, the question that yearns for an answer is, "How do I deal with the fluctuations of adolescence?" There may be many answers to that question, but one that I feel sure will help you is to *cultivate your spirituality*. It's true, having a personal relationship with Jesus Christ not only helps one deal with the emotional turmoil of adolescence, it also helps with the storms of life generally. The prophet Isaiah, speaking of God's ability to provide inner serenity said, *"You will keep in perfect peace all who trust in you, whose thoughts are fixed on you! Trust in the Lord always, for the Lord God is the eternal Rock"* (Isa. 26:3-4, New Living Translation). Not only does having a relationship with God help parents cope with teens, it helps teens cope with themselves! Let me illustrate.

Recently I was visited by two young men selling Christian literature. When I opened the door, I was impressed not as much by the fact that they were selling Christian books as I was by the fact that they were doing it in the dead of winter . . . door to door. They both attended Christian schools, and while out on winter break had taken on the project to help pay their tuition. One was 14 years old and the other 16. They were polite, intelligent and seemed more mature than their ages suggested. I was pleasantly surprised at the level of commitment to their venture, as well as their business savvy. They were not ashamed to talk about their faith, yet they did not force their particular beliefs upon me. Of course, I ended up buying books from them, and as they left I promised to pray for them; characteristically, they promised to do the same for me.

My purpose for sharing that experience is to underscore the point that spirituality is not only beneficial to adults, teens can benefit from it too. Many young people begin to explore matters of faith and religion during the teen years. For some, spirituality becomes a way of life, and they incorporate their knowledge of God into their everyday lives. It helps them deal with the ups and downs of life, because they know they are not alone in the struggle. For others, especially those who grew up in homes where there was no mention of God, no church attendance, or no active faith, developing a spiritual foundation is somewhat of a challenge. It requires looking outside of themselves to believe in a Higher Power, a Creator that loves them unconditionally, but who also holds them accountable for their actions. King Solomon's advice still rings true today: *"Don't let the excitement of youth cause you to forget your Creator. Honor him in your youth before you grow old and no longer enjoy living . . . Yes, remember your Creator now while you are young, before the silver cord of life snaps and the golden bowl is broken"* (Eccl. 12:1, 6a; NLT).

There are many real-life examples of how the development of spirituality during the teenage years can impact adult life, but one in particular comes to mind. Dr. Martin Luther King, Jr. is known all over the world for his contributions to human rights. Right up to his assassination in 1968, he was working tirelessly to help the oppressed, and to raise the nation's awareness of racism in America. Yet, the seed of his convictions were formed early in life. The son of a Baptist minister, King spent much of his early years in the Ebenezer Baptist Church in Atlanta. In fact, the home where he spent the first twelve years of his life was just a block up Auburn Avenue from the church. Later in life, King acknowledged how his attitudes were shaped by his father, "who always put his family first" and his mother, who was "behind the scenes setting forth those motherly cares, the lack of which leaves a missing link in life."[12]

Without a doubt, King's upbringing helped forge his values and belief system, which ultimately had a profound impact on the world. This foundation of faith also helped him weather the storms of the Civil Rights Movement, when criticism and opposition weighed heavily upon his soul. Your child may not become a world leader, but he or she can weather the storms of life by cultivating a relationship with Jesus Christ. The benefits of having such a relationship should never be underestimated.

Another example is found again in the life of Cassie Bernall, one of the twelve students killed at Columbine High School in 1999. In the book written in Cassie's honor, Misty Bernall, Cassie's mother, shares with us the transformation that enabled Cassie to affirm her faith in the face of certain death. She doesn't use the martyr's brush to paint a saintly picture of Cassie, but unashamedly acknowledges the parental struggles she and her husband experienced while Cassie was in High School. However, at some point along the way, the Bernalls made the decision to enroll Cassie in a Christian high school. It was there that Cassie met a friend who invited her to a youth retreat that ultimately changed her life. Following the youth retreat, Cassie's relationship with God flourished and she ceased to be the defiant, rebellious teenager she had once been. In fact, it was Cassie's turn-around that led the Bernalls (at Cassie's request) to allow her to attend Columbine. A note written by Cassie the night before she was killed testified to her newfound faith: "P.S. Honestly, I want to live completely for God. It's hard and scary, but totally worth it." [13]

A final word for those parents wrestling with the vacillating emotions of adolescence . . . *patience*. I've referred to the importance of this virtue previously, but I think it's worth repeating. Though difficult to exercise, there is no substitute for it. The secret is in knowing that "This too, will pass." Children do grow out of adolescence, and most of them eventually get to a place in life where they actually appreciate parental discipline. The hard choice is to practice patience when everything inside you tells you to scream, yell and put the child out of his or her misery. Don't get me wrong, anger can serve useful purposes; it's sometimes a necessary part of identifying and resolving conflict. However, uncontrolled anger can lead to broken relationships, damaged self-concept and physical violence. The words of the Apostle James are worth heeding: *"My dear brothers and sisters, be quick to listen, slow to speak, and slow to get angry. Your [excessive] anger can never make things right in God's sight"* (James 1:19-20; Paraphrased).

CHAPTER SEVEN

Parenting Adolescents with Emotional Disturbances

More often than we'd like to hear about it, newspaper and TV headlines tell stories about young people who commit heinous crimes, even mass murder. One of the most recent of those stories was that of the Virginia Tech massacre that occurred on April 16, 2007. What we learned later was that the shooter, Seung-Hui Cho, had a history of mental illness that began in middle school. A similar tragedy occurred in December 2007 when nineteen year-old Robert Hawkins went on a shooting spree in a Nebraska Shopping Mall. It was later reported by CNN that Hawkins had a history of mental illness and had at one time been taking antidepressant medication. The landlady from whom he rented a room stated that he seemed like "a lost puppy."

While we cannot undo the past, perhaps the lesson we can learn from tragedies such as these is to attune ourselves to those around us, and to educate ourselves regarding mental illness and substance abuse so that we can take the necessary steps to get help for our children.

This last chapter will be concerned with adolescents who have (in mental health terminology) Severe Emotional Disturbances. In other words, we're talking about young people with psychiatric disorders or *psychopathology*. It is not within the scope of this chapter to prescribe specific treatments or remedies, neither should the reader attempt to diagnose someone based upon the information provided here; that should be done by a qualified practitioner (e.g., psychiatrist, psychologist, primary care physician, mental health or addiction professional). However, the purpose of this chapter is to de-mystify certain concepts pertaining to mental illness and substance abuse, so that parents can make the determination themselves whether or not to seek professional help for their teenage son or daughter. Let me also point out that the disorders mentioned here are not exhaustive; there are many more conditions that for the sake of brevity are not mentioned here.

To begin, let me say to those parents reading this, that in order to be of help to your teen, you must be willing to acknowledge your child's illness. All too often, parents ignore signs and symptoms of mental illness or addiction because they refuse to believe that this could happen to "my child." Another reason parents are slow to seek professional help is that they believe the acknowledgement that one's child has an addiction or psychiatric disorder infers blame; i.e. that the parent is somehow responsible for the child's condition, or worse yet, may have caused it. The truth is, mental illness and/or addictive disorders are treatable conditions that often have complex etiologies (causes). As with any disease, the worst thing any parent could do is ignore the symptoms and allow the disease to go untreated. The hard choice is to get beyond self-blame and realize that mental illness is no different than physical illness . . . if you're sick you're sick, and the main thing is to get help as soon as possible.

During the course of this discussion I will use the terms psychopathology, mental illness and psychiatric disorder interchangeably. Psychopathology can be defined as the *study of mental disorders, their problems, causes and processes*. The definition of psychopathology also includes the *manifestations* of mental disorders, particularly the resulting impairment and distress that is inflicted upon the sufferer.[14] Mental illness as referred to here pertains to those disorders listed in the DSM-IV (Diagnostic & Statistical Manual of Mental Disorders—Fourth Edition) published by the American Psychiatric Association. I will also refer to something called *Co-occurring Disorders*, conditions in which both mental illness and alcohol/drug addiction co-exist. In the old days, the term used was "dual diagnosis" which is somewhat of a misnomer. I say this because the word "dual" means "two," when in fact many patients suffering from mental illness and addiction may have multiple diagnoses. The important thing to remember here is that when a patient has co-occurring disorders, *both* must be treated, and it is of little clinical significance to argue over which condition (mental illness or addiction) is considered "primary." With this in mind, let's look at some psychiatric disorders that are common among adolescents.

Attention Deficit-Hyperactivity Disorder (ADHD)

Though often associated with younger children, ADHD is more prevalent among teens than many parents suspect. If the condition existed in elementary school and was never identified or treated, it may continue into high school and even adulthood. The characteristic symptoms are inattention, difficulty concentrating or staying on task, distractibility, and impulsivity. The disorder appears to affect more boys than girls, and while these symptoms may describe behaviors common among teens, for those with ADHD the behaviors are persistent, extreme, and truly outside the control of the teen with the disorder. Adolescents with ADHD have a harder time keeping their minds focused for short periods of time without becoming bored or distracted. They are even more impulsive that their non-ADHD peers, and seem incapable of curbing their automatic reactions of acting before they think. If ADHD goes unrecognized and untreated, a teenager can develop low self-esteem, academic underachievement (even failure), and social isolation, which can follow him or her into adulthood.[15]

The good news is that help is available. In terms of treatment methods, **cognitive-behavioral therapy** (CBT) has proven effective with ADHD teens. The basic framework of CBT is to help the client or patient become aware of the extent of his illness, while at the same time teaching him ways to manage it. It works on the premise of correcting faulty schemas (thought patterns), and by increasing the patient's knowledge of how his behavior is self-defeating. Knowledge is power, and the more one knows about his condition, the better able he is to modify his behavior.

In addition to individual and family therapy, pharmacotherapy (use of medication) is also effective. Medications commonly used to treat ADHD include Ritalin, Adderall, Focalin and Dexedrine. It should be noted that these medicines are stimulant-based and have the potential for abuse. Other long-lasting versions include Concerta, Adderall XR and Metadate CD. A fairly new medication, Strattera, is a non-stimulant and has been approved by the FDA for the treatment of ADHD. Most mental health professionals recommend a combination of *both* psychotherapy and pharmacotherapy. Of course, you should consult your physician regarding the medication that would prove most beneficial for your child.

Oppositional Defiant and Conduct Disorder

These two disorders are actually listed as separate disorders in the DSM-IV. However, they are both behavioral disorders characterized by either an inability or unwillingness to follow societal rules or norms. The distinguishing factors include the child's tendency to break societal rules (things that would lead to arrest if an adult committed the act), or social norms (e.g., respect and consideration for others). The former would favor a diagnosis of conduct disorder, and the latter, oppositional defiant disorder.

To further distinguish between the two, the DSM-IV provides a list of diagnostic criteria for Conduct Disorder that includes: (1) Aggression to people and animals, (2) Destruction of property, (3) Deceitfulness or theft, and (4) Serious violation of rules (i.e. running away from home overnight; truancy prior to age 13). In the same vein, the DSM-IV defines Oppositional Defiant Disorder (ODD) as "A pattern of negativistic, hostile, and defiant behavior lasting at least 6 months." Traits of the disorder include temper flare-ups, frequent arguments with adults, refusal to comply with adult requests, and frequent anger and/or vindictiveness. The important thing to remember is that with each of the disorders, the disturbance in behavior causes clinically significant impairment in social, academic or occupational functioning.[16]

In terms of treatment, individual, family and/or group therapy have proven beneficial with behavioral disorders. However, in order for these therapies to work effectively, there must be willing participants (including a parent or guardian). Too often, a parent or guardian will drop a teenager off at the mental health center or doctor's office with the idea that the child should be "fixed" without any parental involvement. Effective treatment does not seek to place blame, but rather seeks to find out what causes the errant behavior and to discover what courses of action can produce effective change. Good treatment often brings families together to resolve family conflict and to heal long-standing emotional pain.

In cases where the safety and well-being of the child or other family members is at stake, the police or juvenile authorities may need to be involved in order to prevent harm to self or others, or to provide a vehicle through which the child can get the help she needs. No parent wants to see his or her child "locked up," but sometimes this is the hard choice a parent must make. It is true that some people change when they see the light, others change when they feel the heat!

Post-traumatic Stress Disorder (PTSD)

PTSD falls into the category of an **anxiety disorder**. The term anxiety is used frequently in our society, and may mean different things depending on the context in which it is used. For purposes here, it refers to a *negative emotional state involving the element of fear or uncertainty*. Of course, we all experience a certain amount of anxiety in life (e.g. before taking a major exam or before speaking to an audience). PTSD is a *severe* state of anxiety in which a person has been exposed to a traumatic event; one in which he or she has experienced the threat of death or serious injury, or witnessed the death or serious injury of another. Symptoms of the disorder include one or more of the following:

- Recurrent, intrusive recollections of the traumatic event
- Recurrent distressing dreams or nightmares related to the event
- Feeling as though the tragedy is re-occurring (i.e. flashbacks, hallucinations, physical reenactment)
- Psychological distress resulting from exposure to situations resembling the traumatic event
- Avoidance of activities, places or people that evoke recollections of the trauma
- Diminished interest or participation in activities once considered significant

- Sense of foreboding (the feeling that life will be cut short or that something bad will happen)
- Sleep disturbance (difficulty falling or staying asleep)
- Difficulty concentrating
- Exaggerated Startle Response (i.e. "jumpy")

The reason I address PTSD is because it is sometimes overlooked as a causal factor in the behavior of adolescents. I remember seeing a young patient some time ago that was referred because of failing grades. She was a pleasant, cooperative child who had been doing well in school up to the time of her visit. Her mother reported that she seemed to have problems concentrating at school. She also had difficulty sleeping, and appeared to have lost interest in activities she once found interesting. Upon interviewing the child alone I discovered that over a year before, she had experienced a traumatic event . . . two in fact.

The child, whom I'll call Christy, began to relay an incident in which she and a friend had gone into a convenience store to buy snacks. A commotion at the check-out counter erupted, and she then witnessed a robber fatally shoot the store clerk. Although the event had occurred over a year prior to her visit, she remembered the details very clearly. Christy relayed another incident in which she and a friend were riding their bicycles, and an automobile suddenly struck her friend. Her friend survived, but the trauma she experienced by watching this event unfold was never dealt with. When I conveyed this information to her mother, she remembered the bicycle incident, but never thought much more about it. She was totally unaware of her daughter's brush with death at the convenience store; the child was simply too afraid to tell her about it. Once the assessment was completed and a diagnosis of PTSD rendered, therapy was begun, and Christy soon regained interest in her usual activities and her grades improved. In this instance, the case of PTSD was with *delayed onset*. That is, the symptoms began to surface at least six months after the tragic events had occurred.

Perhaps more prevalent than PTSD (but with less severe symptoms) is that of *Generalized Anxiety Disorder* or GAD. While there are other characteristics of GAD, the primary trait is that of *excessive worry*. Individuals experiencing GAD will complain of feeling irritable, fatigued, and restless. They may also have difficulty concentrating and/or sleeping. Anti-anxiety medications that fall into the category of *benzodiazepines* are helpful in treating anxiety disorders. However, care must be exercised when taking benzodiazepines because of their potential for abuse. BuSpar (Buspirone) has also proven beneficial. The psychotherapeutic model of Rational Emotive Therapy (RET) has proven effective with anxiety disorders, primarily because it targets irrational thoughts that perpetuate anxiety.

Major Depressive Disorder

It is estimated that over two million adolescents experience a major depressive episode in any given year. Less than half of those will receive any kind of formal treatment. In addition, suicide among teens continues to present a major health concern. In 2004, the Center for Disease Control (CDC) reported an 8 percent rise in the suicide rate among young people ages 10 to 24. What is significant about the statistics for that year is that it represented the largest rise in suicide rates for that age group in 15 years.[17]

While there are variations upon the theme of depression (unipolar depression, dysthymia, bipolar disorder), my intention here is to make the reader aware of some of the symptoms associated with what is often called Major Depression. The DSM-IV lists the following symptoms, of which five or more are needed (occurring over a two-week period) to substantiate a diagnosis of Major Depressive Disorder:

- Persistently sad or irritable mood
- Loss of interest in activities once enjoyed
- Significant change in appetite or body weight
- Difficulty sleeping or over-sleeping
- Psychomotor agitation or retardation (an increase or slowing down of physical movement)
- Loss of energy or fatigue
- Feelings of worthlessness or inappropriate guilt
- Difficulty concentrating
- Recurrent thoughts of death or suicide

Let me say that even if you don't notice five of the above symptoms, that doesn't mean you should wait until your child gets worse! Any of these symptoms could indicate an emotional problem that needs immediate attention. Sometimes simply providing an avenue for your teen to talk to you (or someone she trusts) can ease an emotional burden, and thereby avoid the development of a more serious condition. Let your child know that there is nothing to be ashamed of in seeking professional help. Unfortunately, there are many people in society who continue to label those with mental illness as "crazy" or "insane." If indeed you choose to obtain professional counseling for your teenager; do so discreetly, so as to avoid having her exposed to the insensitivity of her peers.

There are several treatment methods available for depression, and as with most psychiatric disorders, a combination of medication and psychotherapy seems to work best. In terms of psychotropic medications, those that are designed to treat depression fall into three categories: MAOIs (Monoamine Oxidase Inhibitors), TCAs (Tricyclic Antidepressants), and SSRIs (Selective Serotonin Reuptake

Inhibitors). Of the three, the MAOIs are generally underutilized because of concerns over tyramine-induced hypertension (caused by eating certain foods while taking an MAOI). The Tricyclic antidepressants have proven effective in treating depression but can produce unwanted side effects. The SSRIs are also effective, and have the advantage of being virtually non-lethal in overdose; their side effects are relatively benign.[18] Psychotherapy for Major Depression includes Cognitive Behavioral Therapy (CBT), Rational Emotive Therapy (RET) and Family Therapy.

A discussion of Major Depression cannot be concluded without addressing the subject of teen suicide. Each year in the United States thousands of young people take their own lives. According to the American Academy of Child & Adolescent Psychiatry, suicide is the third leading cause of death for young people ages 15 to 24, and the sixth leading cause of death for 5 to 14 year-olds.

The reasons behind teen suicide are as varied as the teenagers themselves. Sometimes parental divorce or the break-up of a relationship with a girlfriend or boyfriend is a contributing factor. Regardless of the specific reasons, there is a common thread of depression that runs through most all incidents of suicide. People who kill themselves, whether teens or adults, reach a point in life where they feel utterly hopeless, and that life is not worth living. In a sense, it is the last desperate cry for help.

While writing this book, I came across a news article about a 13 year-old girl named Megan Meier, who hung herself in October 2006. She became distraught over cruel comments posted on My Space by a 16 year-old "friend". As it turned out, Megan and her friend had fallen out, and to get revenge, the 16 year-old created the fake profile of a boy named "Josh" who established an online relationship with Megan. She eventually ended the relationship with hateful and demeaning words (supposedly made by Josh). Megan was devastated, and although her mother tried to intervene, the damage had already been done. Megan was later found in her bedroom where she had hung herself; she died the following day. Her death was made even more tragic when it was discovered that the 16 year-olds' mother was the mastermind behind the cruel hoax.

The article underscores how feelings of rejection and disappointment can lead to teen suicide. Adolescence is a time when emotions are intense, and relationships with peers are of the utmost importance. It is also a time when teens acquire a sense of self-identity, and it matters a great deal what other people think of them. Parents should recognize this stage of adolescence, and instead of dismissing it as simply a "phase," strive to help create a healthy self-concept by reaffirming their child's worth and being supportive in the midst of teenage disappointment. Parents should also try to see the world through the eyes of their teens, while at the same time showing them how to keep their world in perspective. That is, help them understand that things are not as bad as they may seem, and that the problems in their lives will somehow work themselves out.

While it is not always easy to tell when a teenager may be contemplating suicide, the following signs may be helpful in preventing a child from taking his or her own life:

- Withdrawal or isolation from family and friends
- Rebellious or violent behavior
- Neglect of personal hygiene or appearance
- Noticeable change in eating or sleeping habits
- Verbal comments such as, "You'd be better off without me" or "You won't have to put up with me much longer"
- Loss of interest in activities once enjoyed (sports, going to movies, etc.)
- Physical complaints such as headaches, stomach problems, or chronic fatigue
- Giving away favorite possessions, or throwing away important belongings
- Change in personality (e.g. extremely detached or unusually happy or peaceful)
- Non-responsive to praise or rewards

Any of the above signs warrant closer observation and intervention by a parent, guardian, friend or responsible adult. Any remark or statement concerning suicide or suicidal intent should be taken seriously. It should be noted that the thought or desire to take one's own life is not always intentional. Sometimes it is *sub-intentional* (i.e. self-destructive behavior that is not clearly perceived to end in death, but may in fact do so). An example might be the individual who is diabetic and refuses to take his insulin. At other times suicide may be *unintentional*; that is, the act or behavior is not consciously intended by the victim to end his life. For instance, a teenager may take a handful of pills from two different pill bottles, not knowing that the combination may be lethal.

Regardless of intent, if you suspect that your child or someone you know may be contemplating suicide, seek professional help right away.

Bipolar Disorder

The term *bi*polar refers to the two predominant features of this particular disorder—depression and mania. Mania can be generally defined as a state of hyper-arousal (e.g. racing thoughts or intense goal-directed activity). Although Bipolar Disorder is rare in young children, it can appear in adolescence. It is often under-diagnosed, and may exist concurrently with other disorders such as ADHD, Obsessive-Compulsive Disorder (OCD), or Conduct Disorder.[19]

Bipolar kids can go from one extreme of the emotional scale to the other several times in one day. The challenge for parents of children with bipolar disorder is in knowing how to manage a wide range of emotions. In addition, how does one distinguish the neurobiological behavior of bipolar disorder from that of teenage angst? Even children with the disorder may recognize that something is wrong, but are unable to explain why they behave the way they do. The good news is that treatment is available, though it may take some searching to find the right mixture of pharmacotherapy and psychotherapy.

While there are different forms of bipolar disorder (Bipolar I, Bipolar II, etc.), it is usually treated with a mood stabilizer such as Lithium, or with anticonvulsants such as Tegretol (Carbamazepine) or Depakote (Divalproex Sodium). Lamotrigine (Lamictal) has also proven effective in the treatment of Bioplar Disorder, though some patients report an adverse side effect in the form of an uncomfortable rash. A new generation of antipsychotic medications, e.g. Zyprexa, Risperdal, Seroquel, Abilify and Geodon have proven effective in the treatment and maintenance of bipolar symptoms such as agitation, aggression and impulsivity.[20] However, these mediations are not without side effects. Again, parents should consult a child psychiatrist or qualified mental heath professional to determine which, if any, pharmacological intervention is right for your child.

Psychotic Disorders

For the sake of this discussion I will use the term *psychosis* to refer to a state of mind characterized by delusions and/or hallucinations. That is to say, an individual with a psychotic disorder may become delusional and entertain thoughts of *grandeur* (an exaggerated or unrealistic sense of accomplishment) or *paranoia* (extreme suspiciousness). He or she may also lose touch with reality and hear voices (auditory hallucinations) or see things that aren't real (visual hallucinations). While society mocks such behavior, for the person experiencing these symptoms it is no laughing matter. Let me also say that the information presented here is not all-inclusive. There are other psychotic disorders (e.g. Brief Psychotic Disorder, Schizoaffective Disorder, Delusional Disorder) that are not discussed for the sake of brevity. However, the goal is to make parents aware of the nature of psychotic disorders so they can recognize certain symptoms and seek additional psychiatric help for their children if needed.

The extent to which psychotic disorders can disrupt one's life is poignantly depicted in the movie, *A Beautiful Mind*. In the movie, Russell Crowe plays the role of Professor John Nash, a brilliant mathematician who begins to experience symptoms of **schizophrenia** while a student at Princeton. He manages to finish college, earning a Ph.D. in Mathematics. He later lands a teaching post at MIT; but the illness soon consumes his life to the point where he is institutionalized. He undergoes various types of psychiatric treatment, and with the aid of his wife, begins the long road toward recovery. Initially resistant to treatment, he gradually accepts the reality of his illness and eventually goes on to win the Nobel Prize in Mathematics. The movie not only depicts the struggles of those with schizophrenia, it also leaves one with a sense of hopefulness; that there is life beyond mental illness.

I use this illustration to point out an often-overlooked fact; that severe mental illness can touch the lives of those we least expect—teenagers. While a psychotic disorder like schizophrenia does not generally occur during the teen years, onset has been known to occur in late adolescence. Onset prior to age 13 is rare.[21] The disorder is characterized by delusions, hallucinations, illogical or incoherent speech, disorganized behavior and "affective flattening" (restriction in facial expressions). The impact of a psychotic disorder on a young person can be devastating, especially when you consider the effect it can have on school, family and peer relationships.

Sometimes a psychotic disorder is the result of drug abuse. In those instances it is referred to as **Substance-Induced Psychotic Disorder**. Drugs that can induce psychosis include alcohol, amphetamines (e.g. "Crystal Meth"), inhalants (gasoline, hairspray, ether, etc.), hallucinogens (PCP, LSD, Ecstasy) and others. I will address substance abuse in more detail near the end of this chapter.

Whether substance-induced or not, psychotic disorders must be treated. Medications like Haldol, Risperdal, Clozaril, Seroquel and Zyprexa have proven beneficial in treating persons with psychotic disorders. The difference in treating substance-induced disorders and non-substance-induced psychotic disorders lies in the approach. For substance-induced disorders, stabilization is often required along with detoxification, depending on the substance used. This is generally done in a hospital setting. Some drugs leave lasting effects even after the substance use has stopped. Crystal methamphetamine (street named "Ice") is one of these. Patients can experience severe paranoia and delusions months after ceasing to use the drug.

When substance abuse and mental illness disorders co-exist, they are considered *Co-occurring disorders*. Traditional approaches to treating persons with co-occurring disorders have resulted in a kind of pigeonholing effect. Many clinicians seek to identify a primary condition that deserves more attention than the other. While this may make sense in theory, in practice *both* conditions must be treated, and it matters less which one is considered "primary." According to Dr. Kenneth Minkoff, one of the leading experts in the field of Co-occurring Disorders, the key to recovery for many people suffering from the diseases of addiction *and* mental illness is the existence of "empathic, hopeful, integrated and continuing relationships."

In other words, treatment professionals must be willing to walk in their patients' shoes, to try to understand the nature of their illnesses and the struggles inherent in trying to get better. All too often, the paternalistic attitude of some in the health care field leads to disregard for the thoughts and feelings of the very patients they are trying to help. People are different, and the prescription that works for one may not work for another. Treatment professionals must also provide hope for their patients; the idea that things can get better. I'm not suggesting giving out *false hope*, but where there is a chance, however slim, that life can improve for the patient, it should be offered. I have found that most people will rise to the expectations we have of them, if we are willing to look beyond immediate circumstances to see possibilities. This concept is not only applicable to treatment professionals; it can be applied to parenting as well. Setting goals for your child and letting them know what you expect of them can motivate them to reach their full potential.

Substance Abuse Disorders

A recent report published by the Substance Abuse and Mental Health Services Administration (SAMHSA) indicated that, on an average day in America, nearly 1.2 million adolescents ages 12-17 smoke cigarettes, 631,000 drink alcohol, 586,000 use marijuana, 50,000 use hallucinogens, 13,000 use cocaine and 3800 use heroin. While other studies have shown progress in terms of decreasing levels of substance abuse among teenagers, this report reminds us that many young people are still engaging in risky behavior.[22]

While it is understandable that teenagers will experiment with drugs and alcohol, it is still a parent's responsibility to convey their expectations regarding alcohol and drug use. It is not realistic to expect teens to avoid illicit drugs when their parents abuse prescription medications. It should also be no surprise to discover that someone's son or daughter is addicted to marijuana when their parents introduced them to it. Children, especially teenagers, simply don't buy the "Do as I *say*" routine; they are too busy watching what their parents do!

For the sake of clarification, the DSM-IV distinguishes between *substance abuse* and *substance dependence*. Abuse involves recurrent use of a substance that leads to problems at home, school or work, including legal problems or problems with interpersonal relationships. Dependence encompasses the above definition, but adds the elements of **tolerance** and **withdrawal**. That is, the person using the substance finds that it takes increasingly larger amounts of it to produce the desired effect or "high." Withdrawal is the body's physical reaction to the absence of a particular substance. Withdrawal symptoms vary depending on the substance used. The definition of Dependence also includes the inability to quit using despite the desire to do so, and the worsening of existing medical conditions despite the user's knowledge that the drug is doing just that. Listed below are substances that are commonly abused by teens and the impact that those substances can have upon them.

Alcohol

One of the oldest and most widely used drugs, alcohol is considered the primary drug of choice for many teens in America today. According to the National Institute on Drug Abuse, about 80 percent of teens drink alcohol. While it is understood that teens will experiment with alcohol and other drugs during adolescence, the slippery slope that leads to chemical dependence is often overlooked.

One young woman recently admitted to me her affinity for alcohol. Influenced by older cousins and other family members, she began drinking in her early teens and soon became a heavy drinker. Enrolled in a job-training program that prohibited the use or possession of alcohol, she realized how difficult it was to stop. Over time, she had become psychologically and physiologically dependent upon alcohol.

The drinking of alcoholic beverages is socially acceptable in our culture; added to that, it can be purchased legally. This does not erase the negative consequences that are associated with alcohol consumption. It is estimated that over three million teenagers are alcoholics (alcohol-dependent), and several million more have a serious drinking problem with which they need help. In addition, alcohol use is linked to the three leading causes of death for 15 to 24 year-olds—auto crashes, homicides and suicides.[23]

So what is a parent or concerned adult to do? The following suggestions may prove helpful in determining if your child has a problem with alcohol:

- **Pay attention to body odors**. Alcohol has a way of seeping through the pores of the skin. If your teen is consuming too much alcohol, his body will give it away.
- **Be a "greeter"**. When your teens come home from a party or outing, even if it's late, make it a point to greet them at the door. This gives you the opportunity to look into their eyes for signs of redness, to smell the odor of alcohol on breath, or to detect any slurring of speech or unsteady gait.
- **Be honest**. If the teen(s) in your life drink and you know it, tell them so. At the same time, tell them that you expect them to behave responsibly, that they shouldn't drink and drive, or for that matter, even ride with someone who is intoxicated. Make them aware of the health risks associated with prolonged alcohol consumption, such as cirrhosis of the liver and impaired cognitive functioning. Let them know also that you are prepared to place restrictions on their freedom if they drink irresponsibly or fail to meet your expectations. While the goal is abstinence, you must realize that you cannot control your teenager's actions 24 hours a day, seven days a week.

Marijuana

Known as *Cannabis Sativa*, marijuana is a widely used psychoactive substance. It is usually smoked in cigarette or cigar fashion (i.e. "joints" or "blunts"), and users report a variety of effects, such as a mellow, problem-free state of mind, unusual giddiness, and a heightened sense of camaraderie. In fact, many users, especially teenagers, believe that marijuana is harmless. This idea is bolstered by the fact that it is culturally acceptable. In some communities, marijuana is as much a part of the social landscape as alcohol is in others. Recent statistics appear to support this. According to the National Clearinghouse for Alcohol & Drug Abuse, over two million Americans used marijuana in the year 2000.

The truth is, marijuana is *not* harmless. Long-term, frequent marijuana use has been linked to depression and psychosis. A recent study conducted by the John A. Burns School of Medicine at the University of Hawaii revealed an increase in risk factors (especially among women) for contracting Adult Onset Glioma, a type of malignant brain tumor.

The active ingredient in marijuana, tetrahydrocannabinol (THC), affects the nerve cells in the part of the brain where memories are formed. This explains why many users report problems with short-term memory loss. Many teenagers develop *Amotivational Syndrome*, a condition in which they become lethargic and lose interest in the important activities of life. As a result, academic performance suffers and school progress is stifled. Signs of marijuana use include impaired attention, bloodshot eyes, increased appetite (the "munchies") and impaired judgment.

Hallucinogens

Hallucinogens derive their name from the fact that they produce *hallucinations*, an altered state of consciousness characterized by changes in sensory perception. The hallucinations produced by drugs in this class are **visual** (seeing things that aren't real), **auditory** (hearing sounds, noises or voices), or **tactile** (e.g. "crawling" sensations on skin).

Drugs in this category include *LSD* (lysergic acid diethylamide), *Psilocybin Mushrooms* (often called "shrooms"), Mescaline (from the cactus plant), and *Phencyclidine* (PCP or "Angel Dust"). A hallucinogenic high or "trip" may last several hours to several days. Some users experience "flashbacks" (i.e., images and feelings of a bad trip that returns unexpectedly). In addition, chronic users can develop persistent perceptual problems as well as depressed moods and panic attacks.

Ketamine (often called "Special K") is pharmacologically similar to PCP, and is used primarily in veterinary medicine as a fast-acting anesthetic. Ketamine can be taken orally, injected intramuscularly (into muscle tissue), or smoked like crack-cocaine. The liquid form is sometimes added to a person's drink, and produces a kind of delirium accompanied by the inability to move, feel pain, or remember events that transpired while under the drug's influence.[24]

Stimulants

This category of drugs derives its name from the fact that they initially stimulate or "speed up" the activity of the central nervous system. Drugs in this class include cocaine and amphetamines. **Cocaine**, for instance, is a widely used stimulant that has ruined many lives, irrespective of social class or race. In its powdered form, it is usually snorted through the nostrils and provides users with a sense of heightened confidence and increased energy.

Crack cocaine is a smokable form of cocaine made by dissolving powdered cocaine in a solution of water and baking soda (or sometimes ammonia and water). The mixture is then boiled until a solid substance rises to the top. This solidified substance is then removed and cooled until it dries, at which time it is cut into pieces or "rocks." Crack-rocks are generally sold on the street in increments of $5 to $20. Signs of use include blurred vision, twitching and fever. Prolonged use results in something called the "cocaine crash," a period of depression that follows cessation of use. Crack-cocaine addicts have also been known to become extremely aggressive and paranoid.

Crystal methamphetamine (often called "Crystal-meth" or "Ice") is a crystallized form of d-methamphetamine. It is produced illegally in homemade labs across the United States from common products such as Lithium (obtained from batteries), Anhydrous Nitrate, Ephedrine, Antifreeze and Lantern fuel. It is usually smoked through a pipe and provides a "rush" that lasts 20-40 minutes. However, prolonged use can produce highs that last up to three days. Signs of use include nervousness, incessant talking, extreme moodiness or irritability, trichotillomania (recurrent hair pulling), and sleep disturbance. Chronic abuse or addiction can lead to depression, severe weight loss, aggression and psychosis (delusions and paranoia).

Ecstasy or **MDMA** (methylenedioxy-methamphetamine) is a "designer drug" that has both hallucinogenic and stimulant properties. The drug is popular within the rave culture and in dance clubs. Also known as the "feel good" drug, it reduces inhibitions, eliminates anxiety, and suppresses the need to eat or sleep. This enables users to party for extended periods of time. Persistent use can cause depression, sleep disorders, paranoia and aggressive behavior.[25]

Inhalants

Another, often overlooked category of abused drugs is that of inhalants. According to the National Clearinghouse for Alcohol and Drug Information

(NCADI), nearly as many 8th graders have tried inhalants as have tried marijuana (18 percent). Yet, fewer than 1 in 20 parents believe their children may have ever abused inhalants. Perhaps one of the reasons so many parents are in the dark when it comes to inhalant abuse is that the chemicals abused are right under their own noses . . . literally. Huffing, sniffing or "bagging" (inhaling from a plastic bag) involves common household chemicals such as glue, paint or paint products, gasoline, nail polish remover, lighter fluid, hair spray, deodorizers and cleaning agents.

The inherent danger of inhalant abuse lies in the fact that all inhalants are absorbed through the lungs and spread to the brain within minutes. One of the most serious risks associated with inhalants is that of *sudden sniffing death*. When a toxic inhalant fills the lungs, it prevents the user from getting sufficient oxygen in the lungs. The resulting deprivation of needed oxygen can lead to heart failure.[26] I recall one such case that involved a teenager who was found dead in his bedroom after inhaling the aerosol Dust Remover. His father, a police officer, never suspected his son of inhalant abuse. He assumed the aerosol cans he found lying around were being used for benign purposes. Other health risks connected with inhalant abuse include impaired judgment, confusion, brain damage, delirium, nausea and vomiting, weight loss and problems concentrating or paying attention.

Narcotics

This category includes drugs derived from the Opium poppy, which is the key ingredient in narcotics. The term *narcotics* stems from the root word "narco" which means "sleep." It is an apt description, since many of the drugs in this class decrease heart and respiration rates, and induce drowsiness. In addition to these effects, long-term use can result in addiction (both physical and psychological), mood swings, seizures, menstrual problems and coma. The DSM-IV refers to drugs in this class as *Opioids*, referring to the fact that many narcotics are synthetic versions of the natural opiates, Morphine, Codeine and Thebaine, all of which are found in Opium.

Heroin is perhaps the most widely used and most addictive of the opiates. It is processed from Morphine, a naturally occurring substance extracted from the seed-pod of certain poppy plants. Pure heroin is white, but after other substances are added (sugar, starch, quinine, etc.) it can turn dark brown. Depending on its form, it can be injected into veins, sniffed ("snorted"), or smoked. Other drugs in the opioid category include prescription painkillers such as OxyContin, Percocet, Demerol and Vicodin. While these drugs are helpful in alleviating severe pain, they have the potential for abuse. Once the body becomes dependent on the medication, the absence of the drug brings on *withdrawal symptoms*.

That is, if an individual tries to stop taking the medication abruptly, negative effects such as vomiting, diarrhea, sleeplessness, anxiety, and muscle aches and pains develop.

Nicotine and Caffeine

As mentioned earlier, recent statistics indicate that in the U.S., approximately 1.2 million adolescents smoke cigarettes. The large number is due in part because young people are not aware of the addictive nature of nicotine when they begin smoking. What begins as a status symbol of anticipated adulthood soon becomes the proverbial millstone around the neck, causing them to sink deeper and deeper into nicotine addiction.

Like any drug with addictive properties, nicotine can produce a dependency that can be both psychological and physiological. Nicotine Dependence becomes evident if, after tying to quit smoking, the user begins to experience withdrawal symptoms that include, but are not limited to, the following physical and mental symptoms:

- Anger and Mood Swings
- Anxiety and Frustration
- Drowsiness or Fatigue
- Headaches
- Insomnia
- Irritability
- Difficulty Concentrating
- Increased Appetite
- Cravings for Cigarettes
- Depression

Of course, most teens smoke away from home, so parents are often unaware that a problem exists. Parents who smoke are sometimes more tolerant of their teenager's smoking habit, and don't really push the issue. Others nag their teens about quitting, while at the same time lighting up in front of them. Needless to say, the message gets lost somewhere in the smoke.

But there is hope for teenage smokers. To help curb nicotine cravings, medication is available in the form of nicotine gum or patches. Other methods of quitting include the HALT Method (i.e., avoid becoming **H**ungry, **A**ngry, **L**onely or **T**ired; triggers associated with smoking), the Buddy System (soliciting the help of a friend who has or is trying to quit smoking), and Oral Substitution (use of candy, gum or mints to assuage the craving for a cigarette). For sure, scolding your adolescent son or daughter in hopes that they will quit seldom works, primarily because nicotine is a highly addictive agent that both stimulates and calms the user. And while many smokers quit "cold turkey," most need medicinal help and/or counseling to kick the habit for good. A better approach to helping your teen quit is to encourage honesty and open communication. Let him know that you're aware of his struggle to quit, and commit to doing all you can to help him stop smoking. I am not suggesting that parents remove boundaries or fail to set limits. If there is to be no smoking in your home, continue to enforce that rule, and enact consequences if the rule if broken. At the same time, remember that addiction of any kind, including nicotine addiction, is fundamentally a "brain disease" that requires time and treatment to overcome.

Caffeine, the other American staple, is not without its addictive properties. In fact, the DSM-IV includes several caffeine-related diagnoses, such as Caffeine Intoxication, Caffeine-Induced Sleep Disorder, and Caffeine-Related Disorder Not Otherwise Specified (for other disorders associated with excessive caffeine use, such as caffeine withdrawal).

It should be noted that "excessive" caffeine use amounts to more than 2-3 cups of brewed coffee per day. However, caffeine is all around us, in our sodas, headache powders, and "energy" drinks. Over-the-counter medications like *No Doz* also contain caffeine, and cases have been reported that compare a severe overdose of *No Doz* to a bad trip on LSD. In a study presented to the American College of Emergency Physicians, researchers found more than 250 cases of medical complications from taking caffeine supplements. Twelve percent of those cases required hospitalization, including the intensive care unit.[27]

The problem is that many teens consider caffeine to be a "harmless" drug, if considered a drug at all. The truth is that any drug taken in excessive amounts can produce harm. Too much caffeine translates into increased heart rate and over-stimulation of the central nervous system. *Caffeine intoxication* occurs when five or more of the following signs appear: Restlessness, nervousness, insomnia, excitement, flushed face, muscle twitching, gastrointestinal disturbances (stomach problems), rambling speech, tachycardia (increased heart rate), inexhaustibility, diuresis (frequent urination) and psychomotor agitation. If you suspect your teenager of caffeine abuse, monitor his or her intake of caffeine, and limit the amount of caffeinated beverages in your home. Substitute colas and teas with fruit juice, lemonade, and non-caffeinated beverages.

Treatment Strategies for Substance Use Disorders

There are various treatment methods available for those suffering from addictive disorders. The most common involve self-help groups based on the Twelve Steps, principles of recovery espoused by Alcoholics Anonymous (AA) and Narcotics Anonymous (NA).[28] The effectiveness of Twelve Step programs lies in the concept of peer motivation. Those seeking deliverance from alcoholism or drug addiction find strength in the support of others who have overcome their addictions. They also find that the AA or NA meetings provide a sense of belonging, a place they can go where they are not judged or criticized harshly.

The power of this kind of support should not be under-estimated, especially when one considers the fact that most addicts have either sabotaged or destroyed the meaningful relationships in their lives, and they welcome the opportunity to be a part of the kind of fellowship that AA or NA provides.

In terms of pharmacological interventions, treatment is determined by the user's drug of choice and the severity of withdrawal. In treating cocaine and amphetamine addiction, for instance, emphasis is on alleviating withdrawal symptoms such as depression. Standard antidepressant mediations are used for this purpose, although the full effects of these medications may not be realized for several weeks. Later in the post-withdrawal phase, however, antidepressants can reduce cravings and increase the abstinence rate.[29] Alcohol withdrawal symptoms generally peak about 72 hours after the last use of alcohol, and benzodiazepines are often used to treat delirium tremens ("shakes") associated with alcohol withdrawal. In the case of opiate withdrawal (i.e. heroin, methadone, oxycontin), buprenorphine has proven effective in minimizing the discomfort associated with detoxing from these highly addictive drugs.[30]

Psychotherapy and counseling are also essential components of recovery for those struggling with addiction. There are different modes of therapy available, including Reality Therapy, Motivational Enhancement Therapy, Dialectical Behavior Therapy, and others. Most substance abuse treatment centers utilize group therapy as an essential treatment tool. The group counseling method provides for the element of catharsis while at the same time providing a safe, supportive environment. Group participants often find strength and hope while listening to others share their life experiences, both good and bad. In terms of individual counseling or psychotherapy, the effectiveness of the process lies in the openness of the recovering person and the professional expertise of the counselor. In general, the more experience and professional training the counselor has, the more effective the outcome.

Whatever treatment modality is used, the important thing is to get help. As the saying goes, "treatment works!" However, barriers of denial and rationalization must often be overcome in order for treatment to be successful. As stated in the tradition of the Twelve Steps, one must first acknowledge that there *is* a problem, and that life has become unmanageable as a result of it. It is only then that doors of healing will open in order for true recovery to take place.

Epilogue

A Final Word

Parenting is no doubt one of the most difficult jobs around . . . and one of the most rewarding. The reward of seeing your child blossom into a productive and caring member of society can't be compared to silver and gold. And yet, that reward often comes at a cost; the cost of many years of self-sacrificing, teaching, admonishing, disciplining, and yes, *hard choices*. But if you cared enough about your teenager to pick up this book, then half the battle is already won.

You see, I believe parents who are willing to learn more about the art of parenting, and who are also willing to amend their ways and try something different in order to be effective as parents are the real heroes of the struggle. For it is not easy to cast aside all the learned parenting behaviors and social rules thrust upon us by our own parents. That is not to say that their methods were bad or totally ineffective. What I *am* saying is that no two children are alike, and some of the parenting methods of previous generations may not be as effective today.

This book was written primarily for the parents and guardians of teenage children. However, I also wrote it for the children themselves. Most of you would agree that teens and young adults face many difficulties growing up in America today, and those difficulties are compounded by issues of abuse, neglect and a general lack of compassion among some parents. Even as I write, there are young people trying to survive in this world without good parents, or without parents at all. There are teenagers who, through no fault of their own, are constantly yelled at, cursed out, ill fed and ill clothed; even homeless. Nevertheless, at the end of the day, many of them will tell you that they still love their parents. If this book helps restore a broken relationship between parent and child, or causes a good parent to become an even better one, it will have been well worth the writing.

ENDNOTES

1 TIME Magazine; July 2004, pg. 60.
2 Spinks, Sarah, Frontline Article: *Adolescent Brains are Works in Progress, www.pbs. org*, 2005.
3 Halgin, R. P. & Whitbourne, S.K. (2000). *Abnormal Psychology: Clinical Perspectives on Psychological Disorders*, pp. 404, 405.
4 Proverbs 14:29, The Open Bible (NKJV); pg. 636.
5 Beder, Sharon, *A Community View: Caring for Children in the Media Age*. New College Institute for Values Research (1998); p. 110.
6 Roiphe, Katie, *Leap of Faith*, Family Circle Magazine; April 1, 2000, pg. 116.
7 Bernall, Misty, *She Said Yes: The Unlikely Martyrdom of Cassie Bernall;* Plough Publishing (1999), pp. 51-52.
8 Larson, Bob, *Extreme Evil-Kids Killing Kids*. Thomas Nelson Inc., 1999, pg.60.
9 Internet Article: *Measuring Student Behavior*, Pride Surveys (2005); *www. pridesurveys.com*
10 Proverbs 22:6, The Open Bible (NKJV); Thomas Nelson Publishers; pg. 644.
11 Ephesians 6:4, The Life Recovery Bible (NLT); Tyndale House Publishers; pg. 1429.
12 Carson, Clayborne & Holloran, Peter: *A Knock At Midnight*, Warner Books (1998); pg ix.
13 Bernall, Misty, *She Said Yes: The Unlikely Martyrdom of Cassie Bernall;* Plough Publishing (1999), Preface.
14 Maxmen, Jerrold S. & Ward, Nicholas G., *Essential Psychopathology and Its Treatment*, Norton Publishing (1995); pg. 5.
15 Internet Article: *Your Adolescent—Attention Deficit/Hyperactivity Disorder*, American Academy of Child & Adolescent Psychiatry, *www.aacap.org*, 2008, pg. 2.
16 DSM-IV-TR (Diagnostic & Statistical Manual of Mental Disorders-Desk Reference); American Psychiatric Assn., (2000); pg. 69.
17 Internet Article: *CDC: Suicide Rate Jumps for Kids*, MSNBC News Service, Retrieved 9/7/07; *www.msnbc.com*
18 Koocher, Gerald P. & Norcross, John C., *The Psychologists' Desk Reference*; Oxford University Press (2005); pg. 454.
19 Greenberg, Rosalie, *Bipolar Kids: Helping Your Child Find Calm in the Mood Storm;* Da Capo Press (2007), pg. xiii.
20 Ibid, pg 163.

21   Internet Article: *Early Onset Schizohrenia*. Retrieved 3/5/08; reviewed by Julia Tossell, MD, *www.nami.org*

22   Press Release: *New Report Provides Startling Look at Substance Abuse On An Average Day in the Life of American Adolescents*, SAMHSA, Released Oct. 18, 2007; *www.samhsa.gov*

23   Internet Article: *Alcohol and Teen Drinking*, Focus Adolescent Services; 2007, *www.focusas.com*

24   Source: *Street Drugs: A Drug Identification Guide*, Publishers Group, LLC; 2004, pg. 52

25   Ibid; pp. 25-26.

26   Internet Article: *Huffing—Inhalant Use*. Retrieved 12/18/07, *www.psychiatric-disorders.com*

27   Deardorff, Julie, *Caffeine Abuse: An Emerging Problem*, posted November 21, 2006; *www.chicagotribune.com*

28   Internet Article: *12 Steps of Alcoholics Anonymous*; Retrieved 4/10/08, *www.12steptreatmentcentres.com*

29   Goldstein, Avram, Addiction: From Biology to Drug Policy; Oxford University Press (2001); pg. 187.

30   1nternet Article: *Opiate Detox for Heroin and Opiate Dependence*, Retrieved 4/10/08; *www.drug-rehabilitation.com/opiate-detox*

www.ingramcontent.com/pod-product-compliance
Lightning Source LLC
Chambersburg PA
CBHW021302280526
45784CB00005B/2477